THE NEW PLANT LIBRARY

DAHLIAS

THE NEW PLANT LIBRARY

DAHLIAS

TED COLLINS

Photography by Jonathan Buckley

LORENZ BOOKS

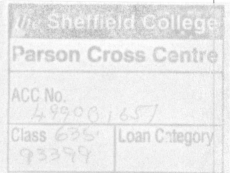

...ublished in 2000 by Lorenz Books

Lorenz Books is an imprint of
Anness Publishing Limited
Hermes House
88–89 Blackfriars Road
London SE1 8HA

This edition published in Canada by Lorenz Books,
distributed by Raincoast Books Distribution Limited,
8680 Cambie Street, Vancouver, British Columbia V6P 6M9

Published in the USA by Lorenz Books, Anness Publishing Inc.,
27 West 20th Street, New York, NY 10011; (800) 354 9657

A CIP catalogue record for this book is available from the British Library

Publisher Joanna Lorenz
Project Editor Polly Willis
Designer Dave Jones
Photographer Jonathan Buckley

1 3 5 7 9 10 8 6 4 2

■ HALF TITLE PAGE
'David Howard'
■ FRONTISPIECE
'Peachette'
■ TITLE PAGE
'Minley Carol'

■ LEFT
'Hamari Gold'
■ OPPOSITE LEFT
'Glorie van Heemstede'
■ OPPOSITE RIGHT
'Lismore Willie'

Contents

Introduction

*D*ahlias are well-established favourites among gardeners. A never-ending range of colour, size and form makes them a must for gardens of any size. Unrivalled for cut flower use, they are also paramount in the colourful contribution they make to the overall beauty of the garden, blooming profusely during the summer and autumn. Despite their exotic appearance, dahlias are easy to grow, taking nature's hard knocks and rarely failing to deliver perfect blooms, new growth and tubers for the following year's plants.

This book offers both spectacular colour photographs and concise practical advice on successful cultivation, as well as information on types, propagation, pests and raising new varieties. Listing details of over 70 varieties, it will provide both beginner and established grower with a view of the best of what is available.

There is also a useful seasonal calendar to provide a reminder of what to do and when to do it for best results and a useful list of nurseries and dahlia societies so that you can pursue your interest further in these spectacular plants.

■ RIGHT
'Jescot Julie', a double-orchid type, provides some eye-catching colour.

The world of dahlias

■ BELOW
Dahlias in their late-summer glory: at this
time of year blooms are at their best.

To the average gardener a dahlia is
simply a dahlia. In fact dahlias are
star performers, perhaps the most
versatile of flowers, coming in so
many diverse forms and colours.
They are invaluable in the garden,
providing a spectacular display in
borders and beds, and as cut flowers
for use in the home or office.

They are also the backbone of
local flower shows and feature
majestically in parks and public
gardens throughout the world.

Types of dahlia

Dahlia flowers, which can be as large
as a dinner plate or as small as a
cherry, are classified according to
their shape. The main groups are
single, anemone, orchid, collerette,
waterlily, decorative, ball, pompon,
cactus and miscellaneous, with
various further subdivisions. Dahlias
can be virtually any colour through
shades of white, yellow, orange,
bronze, flame, red, pink, lilac, purple

and even bi-colours of all mixes,
although as yet no truly blue variety
has been raised. A connoisseur of
dahlias is always looking for perfect,
symmetrical blooms, each type having
a recommended shape.

Over many years of growing
dahlias, there are so many excellent
varieties to choose from. Of all these,
'Moorplace', a purple pompon dahlia
raised in the United Kingdom in 1957
(named after the Surrey golf course),
and 'Kidd's Climax', a pink giant-

■ BELOW
**To stop the heavy blooms being damaged,
stakes are used to support the plants.**

flowered decorative dahlia raised in
New Zealand in 1940, are still as fresh
today as when they were first grown.
Pompons should be 5cm (2in)
spheres, sitting fully on top of their
stems, like drumsticks. Giant-flowered
decoratives by definition are big, really
big: a bloom can be as much as 45cm
(18in) in diameter and 30cm (12in) in
depth. Between these two extremes
there is a wide variety of size and
shape, with something to suit
everyone. There are spiky cactus types
such as 'Kiwi Gloria', a small-
flowered dahlia that is lilac-and-
white, the queen of the show bench.
'Glorie van Heemstede', a pure

yellow waterlily decorative type, is
unbeatable as a cut flower. 'Giraffe',
a yellow-and-bronze variegated
double orchid type, is much sought
after for floral art.

Trials and societies

Dahlias grow well in both the
northern and southern hemispheres.
In the United Kingdom, the National
Dahlia Society holds trials of
established varieties at the Royal

■ RIGHT
**Pompon dahlias, such as 'Small World',
produce an abundant display.**

■ BELOW
'Witteman's Superb' creates a stunning
effect when combined with delicate,
purple flowers of *Verbena bonariensis*.

Horticultural Society Gardens at
Wisley and at Golden Acre Park,
Leeds (in conjunction with
Gardening Which? magazine) where
new varieties are also trialled. The
Welsh Dahlia Society trial dahlias at
Pencoed College of Horticulture,
Bridgend. The American Dahlia
Society has two major trial gardens:
the Pacific Coast Garden in Lakeside
Park, Oakland, and the Pacific Coast
North-West Garden at Tacoma, as
well as other trial gardens all over the
country, including New York,

Minneapolis, Bonneyville, Spokane,
Georgia, Roseburgh, Cincinnati and
Victoria in British Columbia, Canada.

The New Zealand Dahlia Society
carries out trials at various locations
on both the North and South islands.

Major horticultural events, or
floriades, are held in many European
towns, such as Amsterdam and Padua,
where dahlias figure prominently.
Dates vary annually so if you are
travelling during the flowering season
in Europe, check the local newspapers
for listings of events. In the United

Kingdom, two major dahlia shows are
held in September, at Shepton Mallett
and Harrogate. With more than 130
classes ranging from collections of
huge giants to multitudes of pompons,
these shows are a riot of colour, as
exhibitors arrange their outstanding
blooms. Exhibitors and gardeners
flock to see varieties not seen before in
public, and visitors are drawn from all
over the world.

The USA National is held in a
different major city each year, usually
in a convention or conference centre.

Blooms of outstanding quality are mostly presented singly but with some multi-bloom classes. The event is more than a show, as local parks and nurseries are also visited.

The Seattle Puget Sound Dahlia Society also hosts a major dahlia show. This precedes the USA National show and differs in that it takes place in a shopping mall. Staging blooms, judging and prize-giving all take place with shoppers admiring the 'goodies' on display on the dahlia show bench.

Because New Zealand comprises two islands, the national show alternates yearly between them. New and established varieties are grown to perfection and shown, with friendly rivalry between growers from the North and South islands.

Floral art

Dahlias, with their vibrant colours, strong stems and variation of form, prove a perennial favourite amongst flower arrangers. They feature throughout the year, although more predominantly in the autumn when the blooms are at their best. The most popular varieties are miniature, small decoratives and ball dahlias, while cactus and pompons are also widely used. The variations of displays that can be created using a mixture of type and colour are virtually limitless; striking effects can also be produced by creating a display from a single colour or type. For those wanting to experience the thrill of competition, there are a huge number of clubs and

shows organized by individual flower-arranging societies – contact your local dahlia society for details – at which floral art can be displayed. Visiting shows is a great way for beginners to learn about floral art, as the standard of exhibits is usually very high.

Themes of exhibitions vary from show to show, with some relying more specifically on colour, others on form. Each show will have its own rules, but when arranging flowers for pleasure, you can follow your imagination.

A selection of the best varieties of dahlia to use in arrangements would include: 'Cherida', 'Garden Festival', 'Giraffe', 'Hayley Jane', 'Jescot Julie', 'Karen Glen' and 'Taratahi Lilac'.

The history of dahlias

Dahlias first arrived in Europe from Central America over 300 years ago, although the existence in that part of the world of both single and double bloom varieties was already known to the Europeans in the late 16th century.

The Aztecs called dahlias 'acocotli' or 'cocoxochitl', which meant 'hollow pipes' or 'water tubes', because of their hollow stems. Aztec inscriptions link single dahlia blooms to religious rituals associated with the sun, because of the ray-like petals of the early single varieties. As the Spanish conquistadors explored the sub-tropical mountain slopes of what is now Mexico in search of gold and silver, they came across single-flowered dahlias, which, with their small blooms, differed in appearance to their modern descendants. They sent roots of this as yet unnamed plant back to Spain, perhaps with a thought to it becoming a rival to Drake's newly discovered potato. However, the tubers are no culinary delight, and no one was interested.

Dahlias in Europe

The first dahlia seeds to arrive in Europe are generally believed to have been sent by Vincente de Cervantes (director of the Mexican Botanical Gardens) to Abbé Cavanilles (director of the Madrid Botanical Gardens) in 1789. Cavanilles identified three species of dahlia – *D. pinnata*, *D. coccinea* and *D. merckii*. He named the plants 'dahlia' in honour of his Swedish colleague Anders Dahl. Since Cavanilles was the first

■ LEFT
'East Court', a dwarf single, is used to give interest to a border with *Rudbeckia fulgida speciosa.*

■ BELOW
D. merckii was one of the first varieties
of dahlia that was sent to Europe from
Mexico in the 18th century.

■ BELOW
Decoratives, such as 'Davenport Lesley',
are a good all-round type: they need little
support, and provide colour and shape.

person to study dahlias, had he been
less modest this book might well have
been about 'cavanillias'.

It could also have been about
'georginas' because soon after dahlias
had been named by Cavanilles,
Professor Wildenow of Berlin
attempted to have them renamed
'georgina' in honour of his friend
Professor Georgi of St Petersburg.
This name persisted in parts of
Europe until the 1930s.

According to tradition, Lady
Butte, the wife of the British
ambassador to Spain, brought the
first dahlia seeds to England in the
1790s. These appear to have been
from *D. coccinea*, a scarlet single-
flowered species. Tradition also has it
that plants produced from these seeds
were lost through neglect. Lady
Holland, the wife of another British
ambassador in Madrid, sent seeds
home to England, with
similar results. Horticulturists
continued to obtain seeds
from Spain and propagated
them with
greater success.
Genetic
modification
brought about by
dahlia hybridists –
assisted by local
insects – soon changed

D. coccinea, *D. rosea* and *D. pinnata*
from single blooms with long weak
stems into *D. variabilis*, which had
several rows of ray-florets and was the
forerunner of the fully double dahlias.
Early versions of these were grown
between 1812 and 1814 in the
gardens of a chateau near Paris.
D. superflua, a fully double, purple-
flowered variety, was secured and
heralded the arrival of modern
dahlias; *D. superflua* has been
incorporated into *D. variabilis*.

Thereafter, raisers in the United
Kingdom in the early 19th century
produced a range of dahlias – spotted,
striped and picotes – but virtually all
of these were what we now call 'ball'

dahlias, with a few anemone varieties. At this time, dahlias were grown only by those who were fortunate enough to own or live in large country houses, and tubers changed hands at exorbitant prices – a guinea for established varieties and as much as £100 (several years' wages for an ordinary labourer) for new varieties. Competitions were staged, to encourage nurserymen to work with this exotic plant. During the late 19th century, the 'collerette' types of dahlia were produced in France. Some time afterwards, German growers produced the 'Lilliput' dahlia, whose name was changed in France to 'pompone' dahlia, because of the resemblance it bore to the button on their sailors' hats. This has subsequently been corrupted to the current name, 'pompon'.

In the late 19th century a nurseryman in Utrecht received a batch of tubers from Mexico and an unexpected new variety arrived in the dahlia world. The cactus dahlia, with long, rolled, narrow petals, had been born, although at the time it was named 'Juarezii' in honour of the then Dutch premier. All modern cactus dahlias are its descendants.

Decorative dahlias are descendants of the early peony varieties and were not much liked, when first released. Although given an impetus by the Dutch, it was not until the late 19th century, after German growers had produced giant decoratives with well-formed blooms and stems, that they became acceptable. Dutch growers bred them, producing similar, small- and medium-flowered versions.

Dwarf versions of dahlias were discovered in Mexico in 1750. They were only about 45cm (1ft 6in) high with minute, single blooms. These and their successors are now the only dahlias to produce progeny true to the parent; these are today's 'bedders'. Originally known as 'Tom Thumbs' (later redesignated as 'mignons'), they were single bloomed, later to become fully double. Many of these varieties have extraordinary foliage, ranging from dark brown through to almost black. Modern varieties are effective for garden use, particularly with contrasting red or yellow blooms.

The modern dahlia

The Great Exhibition held in London in 1851 changed the world of the dahlia. People from all social classes visited the Exhibition, beginning the great love affair with the dahlia. The resulting demands on the dahlia raisers led to the explosion of colour and variety of form that we enjoy today. This interest in new varieties did not end in the 19th century. The raising of new dahlias continues in New Zealand, where, recently, some new, exciting developments have been taking place. In the 1980s, a New Zealand raiser visited Mexico and brought back a collection of dahlia species, many previously uncultivated. Research work carried out with the University of Auckland and the Auckland Regional Botanic Garden led to a better understanding of how the cultivated dahlia was developed. In addition, quite new hybrids were created using different species. 'Titoki Point' is the first cultivar to incorporate genes from *D. australis*, and tree dahlias with red flowers have been created by combining *D. apiculta* with *D. coccinea*. A whole new world of dahlias beckons.

In 1881 the National Dahlia Society was founded in London, the first of many specialist national dahlia societies. The New Zealand Society was formed over 60 years ago and the American National Society more than 80 years ago.

Dahlias are now big business throughout the horticultural world: in the United States, Australia, New Zealand and South Africa, as well as the United Kingdom, other European countries and, more recently, India. Perhaps the most successful country since the 1960s has been the Netherlands, with millions of tubers and cut flowers passing through Schiphol auction market and airport.

■ RIGHT
Trial grounds are where new varieties of dahlia are cultivated and developed before they are released for general sale.

The dahlia plant

Petals from the different types.
Left to right: miscellaneous; single; waterlily;
collerette; decorative; semi-cactus; cactus;
fimbriated (laciniated); ball; and pompon.

Dahlias are natural hybrids of unknown parentage, often referred to as *D. pinnata* or *D. variabilis*. It may be that an original parent was a cross between *D. maxonii*, a tree dahlia growing to 5.5m (18ft) with magenta blooms, and *D. coccinea*, which contributed scarlet and orange colouring as well as lower growth. We shall perhaps never know the true parentage although genetic pathology can now reach back into the past. Being polyploids, that is plants containing twice the basic number of chromosomes, dahlias are able to develop new forms that differ from the original parents. Chance matings of wild plants in their Central American homeland have, over the passage of time, resulted in the range of colour and variegation, of form and size of modern dahlias. Dahlias have also lent themselves readily to modern hybridizing experiments.

Structure of the plant

The habit of the dahlia plant is that of a bush. As in most plants, the stem tip contains the hormone auxin. This induces the plant to increase its strong central stem, while side breaks or stems will be weaker, the number of breaks being dependent on the variety. If the central stem is nipped, or 'stopped', stronger lower breaks will occur. Each stem contains three or four pairs of leaves, each pair at a stem node, and usually, if left, a central flower bud and one or two side, auxiliary flower buds. The purpose of any plant's leaves is to facilitate photosynthesis. The leaves absorb carbon dioxide from the air and, with the help of sunlight and the green pigment chlorophyll, this is mixed with water taken up by the root system to produce inulin, a form of sugar used for plant growth.

For healthy plants, therefore, it is essential that each plant has a good balance of root, branch and leaf.

At the end of each growing season any inulin that has not been used by the plant is stored in the tuber (the underground storage organ formed from a swollen root) ready to promote the following year's growth.

Types of dahlia

Dahlias are classified according to the shape and size of their blooms. Each type of dahlia is quite distinct, with some types better suited for exhibiting, others for use in the garden or for cut flowers. The main types of dahlia are illustrated on the following pages.

Some of the types described also exist in giant-flowered versions. These include decoratives, cactus and semi-cactus.

It is possible to produce really large blooms, which are mainly used for show purposes.

To achieve this, growers restrict the number of blooms on each plant to about three while the plant is still developing.

■ LEFT
SINGLE ('MOONFIRE')

The simplest dahlias are the single-flowered types. These have a single row of petals around a central disc of tiny florets. With blooms only 2.5cm (1in) in diameter, these are in the main dwarf bedders, raised from seed or reproduced vegetatively. They only grow to a height of 45cm (18in).

■ RIGHT
ANEMONE ('PASO DOBLE')

The rarest form of dahlia is the anemone-flowered type. The blooms have one or two outer rings of flattened ray-florets surrounding a group of small, tufted tubular florets which cover the central disc. This arrangement makes the bloom resemble a pincushion. Anemone varieties grow to about 90cm (3ft) in height and tend to be used for garden decoration only.

■ LEFT

WATERLILY ('GLORIE VAN HEEMSTEDE')

Waterlily-flowered dahlias are so-called because they resemble a waterlily. In fact they are a type of decorative, full double, with broad, mostly flat ray-florets, but shallower than the normal decorative type. The normal height is up to 1.5m (5ft). The plants are more bushy and blooms are borne on longer, thinner stems than decoratives, making them useful for cut blooms or floral art, but requiring support in wind and rain.

■ RIGHT

COLLERETTE ('CURIOSITY')

Another exotic type are the collerette dahlias. These have an open, central disc, usually with an outer ring of eight ray-florets and a wonderful inner ring of shorter florets (the collar) from which the type takes its French name of collerette. Collerettes are usually about 90cm (3ft) in height and are excellent for cut flower or exhibition use.

■ LEFT

DECORATIVE ('TRENGROVE JILL')

Decorative dahlias are the strongest type. Their fully double blooms, with flat, broad ray-florets, originated from the now defunct peony-flowered dahlia. With powerfully built blooms of great depth and size, some varieties reflect (curve) right back on to their strong stems. There are varieties to serve every purpose: garden flowers, cut bloom and exhibition. Heights vary from 90cm (3ft) to 1.2m (4ft) and support is required.

■ RIGHT

BALL ('AMBER GLOW')

Ball dahlias, descended from the 18th- and early 19th-century show-and-fancy dahlias (those developed for show purposes), perhaps deserve a more elegant name – the ray-florets lie neatly together, like tiles on a roof rather than like a ball. With their strong stems, they make excellent garden and cut flowers and are the mainstays of horticultural shows. About 90cm (3ft) in height, they need support. Ball dahlias make excellent tubers, and are often sold pre-packed at garden centres.

■ LEFT

POMPON ('SMALL WORLD')

Pompon dahlias, spherical beauties of 5cm (2in) in diameter when grown to perfection, are very popular. Each plant is capable of producing a hundred miniature show-and-fancy blooms, resembling drumsticks on strong wiry stems, each one a perfect buttonhole. Easy to grow with minimum support, and reaching up to 90cm (3ft) in height, pompons have been used to create a dahlia 'hedge'.

■ RIGHT

CACTUS ('ALVA'S DORIS')

Cactus blooms are fully double, with long, slender revolt or recurving petals. The tightly rolled petals have a spiky shape, hence the name 'cactus'. These produce an abundance of blooms, excellent for cut flowers, garden borders or exhibition. These flowers are less prone to rain damage than many dahlias. Cactus dahlias grow to 1m (3¼ft) or more in height, and need support.

■ LEFT
SEMI-CACTUS ('HAMARI ACCORD')

Semi-cactus dahlias lie between the cactus and the decorative. They too have long, slender petals, but broader than those of cactus dahlias and only half revolt or recurving. These dahlias have all the advantages of both their cousins and none of their weaknesses, although they are less tolerant of rain than the cactus. Cut, garden or exhibition varieties abound. They grow to 1m (3½ft) and require some support.

■ RIGHT
FIMBRIATED ('NARGOLD')

Both cactus and semi-cactus dahlias have sub-groups of fimbriated (laciniated) dahlias. These have split petals, which in some varieties is so pronounced that they resemble chrysanthemums or carnations. These varieties are becoming increasingly popular.

■ LEFT
MISCELLANEOUS ('JESCOT JULIE')

Miscellaneous dahlias is a term used to describe dahlias that do not come under any of the above described groups. Among these are orchid dahlias much beloved of floral arrangers, as well as what remain of the peony dahlias, truly a feast of form, with variations to suit all horticultural use.

■ RIGHT
GREEN-EYED

'Green-eyed' is the name applied to a fault in a dahlia bloom whereby the centre of the bloom fails to develop properly. The petals in the centre remain green, firm and undeveloped. This is usually due to a lack of water being given to the plant when it is most in need, and some varieties are more susceptible than others. Giving your dahlias plenty of water is vital, but is never more so than when the first green eyes have appeared in the dahlia patch. Here, the green-eyed bloom appears on the right, non-green on the left.

■ LEFT
CLOCK-FACED

The term 'clock-faced' applies to blooms that do not sit correctly on the stem. Ideally, a bloom should sit at 45° to the stem (except pompons which should sit on top). It is also acceptable for other varieties to sit on the stem, but flowers angled more sharply than 45° tend to look less effective. If blooms are for cut flower use or exhibition, nature has to be assisted (this is usually only done with medium, large and giant blooms). Methods used to correct this fault vary, but a common one is to angle the bud from the stem as it develops. Here, the clock-faced bloom appears on the left.

Plant Catalogue

Plants in this catalogue have been listed alphabetically, with the type, colour and height of maximum growth given for each. For more plants, please refer to the Other recommended dahlias section later in the book.

The flower sizes given below correspond to the United Kingdom's National Dahlia Society (NDS) exhibition flowerhead classifications:

Giant: over 25cm (10in)
Large: 20–25cm (8–10in)
Medium: 15–20cm (6–8in)
Small: 10–15cm (4–6in)
Miniature: less than 10cm (4in)
Pompon: less than 5cm (2in)

■ ABOVE
'ALVA'S SUPREME'

Raised by Vic Frost in New Zealand in 1956, this pure yellow giant-flowered decorative has survived the test of time and been a show-winner throughout the world. With strong stems for exhibition, it is easy to grow but late in flowering, and requires an early start, by split tuber if necessary. Grows three blooms per plant only. Prize-winning sports are 'White' (Mills 1979) and 'Cream' (Machin 1990). Grows to a height of about 1.1m (3½ft).

■ LEFT
'ART DECO'

One of the Gallery range of dwarf bedding dahlias produced by Adrian and Cees Verwer in Holland from 1996, this variety is a striking orange with an even deeper orange centre. It is useful for borders or patio pots and for late-season use from late-struck cuttings. Grows to a height of about 25–30cm (10–12in).

■ LEFT
'BELLE OF THE BALL'

A large-flowered semi-cactus raised by Bob Surber in the United States in 1995, that will be around for many years. This lavender-pink dahlia is heavily fimbriated (laciniated), with every petal split for about 2.5cm (1in), which makes it excellent for garden, cut flower or exhibition use. Grows to a height of 1.2m (4ft).

■ BELOW
'BISHOP OF LLANDAFF'

Raised in Wales by I. Treseder in 1928, this low-growing, miscellaneous dahlia has been used ever since in gardens and parks throughout the world. It is prized for its single red petals surrounding an open centre with yellow anthers and dark foliage. It has some resistance to virus. Grows to a height of about 60cm (2ft).

■ ABOVE
'CHARLIE TWO'
(SYN. 'MASCOT MAYA')

'Charlie Two' was raised by E. A. Fuller in 1986, while 'Mascot Maya' was raised by S. Mellen in 1994, both in the United Kingdom. The two varieties, both pure yellow, medium-flowered decorative dahlias, resemble each other so closely when cut blooms are placed side by side that the NDS classification committee concluded they are indistinguishable. The deep blooms are excellent for exhibition work and the plant makes a full bush. Grows to a height of 1.2m (4ft).

'CHIMBORAZO'

Raised by John Crutchfield in Sussex, United Kingdom, in the mid-1970s, this collerette dahlia produces plenty of blooms for show, garden and cut flower use. The flowers are scarlet with a collar tipped in pale yellow. Grows to a height of about 90cm (3ft).

■ RIGHT
'CORNEL'

Introduced by Cor Geerlings of the Netherlands in 1994, this perfectly formed red ball dahlia is excellent for exhibition, garden and cut flower use. It is now classified in the United Kingdom as both a miniature- and a small-flowered ball, but in the United States as a small-flowered ball. As with most red dahlias, back petals bleach in the sun, but they revolve fully to the stem. Grows to a height of 90cm (3ft).

■ ABOVE
'CLAIR DE LUNE'
(SYN. 'MOONLIGHT')

Since its introduction by Dahlia Bruidegom in the Netherlands in 1946, this blended yellow collerette dahlia has stood the test of time. The outer petals are a darker yellow than the collar. It is a strong grower, provides abundant blooms for cut flower and garden use, and produces excellent tubers. Grows to a height of 90cm (3ft).

■ ABOVE
'DAVID HOWARD'

Evident in most United Kingdom municipal or stately home gardens in which dahlias are grown, this distinctive miniature-flowered decorative was raised by David Howard of the United Kingdom in 1965. The dark coppery-coloured foliage sets off the orange-bronze blooms to great advantage. Requiring little or no support, it is invaluable for garden bedding either as edging or for mixing in herbaceous borders. Grows to a height of 75cm (2½ft).

■ RIGHT
'DORIS DAY'

Named by Mijnheer Weijers of the Netherlands in 1952, this dark red, small-flowered cactus dahlia lives up to its star billing as a garden and cut flower variety but it loses out on the exhibition bench because it produces green bracts, or small petaloides, between the petals. It was considered to be one of the finest cut flowers of its day. This dahlia forms a compact bush, which looks spectacular when the blooms are at their best. Grows to a height of 90cm (3ft).

■ ABOVE

'ELLEN HUSTON'

Raised in Canada by Earle Huston, and introduced in 1975, this superb orange-red dwarf bedding dahlia with dark foliage needs no support. It will fit into any herbaceous or mixed border, and can be combined with 'David Howard' to great effect. Grows to a height of 45cm (18in).

■ BELOW

'EASTWOOD MOONLIGHT'

Introduced by John Sharp in the United Kingdom in 1975, this is a superb medium-flowered, semi-cactus variety that is widely used for garden, cut flower or exhibition purposes. It has well-formed, pure yellow blooms on the end of long stems. Care should be taken when growing it for exhibition, as it can be very susceptible to marking in seasons of mists and heavy dews. Grows into a compact bush. Sports include 'White Moonlight', 'Lauren's' and 'Pim's'. Grows to a height of 1.1m (3½ft).

■ ABOVE

'FASCINATION'

Raised by Elsdon in the United Kingdom in 1964, this low-growing, miscellaneous peony dahlia has stood the test of time as a garden variety. Purple-flowered with dark bronze foliage, it grows to a height of 60cm (2ft).

■ LEFT
'FIDALGO CLIMAX'

Raised by Dick Matthies in the United States and introduced as a variety in 1994, this is a large, semi-cactus dahlia. When it was first introduced, it was considered by many as being the top fimbriated (laciniated) dahlia in the United States. It has bright, pure yellow, deep blooms on good, strong stems, and really is one for the exhibitor. Grows to a height of 1.1m (3½ ft).

■ RIGHT
'FIGURINE'

This is a fine, small-flowered waterlily dahlia that originates from Australia. It was raised by W. Tapley in 1992, and is wonderfully easy to grow. The masses of pink-and-white blended blooms on long straight strong stems are excellent for garden use, and as cut flowers. Grows to a height of 1.2m (4ft).

■ ABOVE

'FIRE MOUNTAIN'

This miniature-flowered, decorative dahlia was introduced
by Walter Jack, Belle Fleur Gardens, New Zealand, in
1985. With bright red blooms on black foliage, it has proved
to be an outstanding dahlia for garden use. Grows to a height
of 1.1m (3½ft).

■ RIGHT

'GLORIE VAN HEEMSTEDE'

Among the first of the modern waterlily dahlias, this pure
yellow variety was raised by Bakker in the Netherlands in
1947. It is excellent for garden and cut flower use and in
exhibitions can still win against more recent waterlily varieties.
Grows to a height of 90cm (3ft).

■ ABOVE
'HAMARI ACCORD'

'Hamari' is Hindi for 'our house' and is the prefix used for a long line of dahlias raised by Walter 'Pi' Ensum, one of the greatest dahlia breeders in the United Kingdom. This pure yellow, large-flowered semi-cactus dahlia was raised in 1986; it has since dominated exhibitions worldwide. Grows to a height of 1.2m (4ft).

■ ABOVE
'HAYLEY JANE'

A non-stop and prolific provider of blooms, this striking small-flowered, semi-cactus dahlia was raised by G. Tichard in the United Kingdom in 1978. Bearing purple-tipped white blooms, it is an excellent cut flower and good for garden display, if somewhat tall. Grows to a height of 1.2m (4ft).

■ LEFT
'HAMARI GOLD'

This giant-flowered decorative dahlia was raised by Walter 'Pi' Ensum in the United Kingdom and introduced in 1984. With huge golden-bronze blooms on strong stems, it was unbeaten in its day with three blooms being grown per plant. Makes a good garden flower if unrestricted. Grows to a height of 90cm (3ft).

■ LEFT

'HILLCREST REGAL'

This is a relatively recent introduction which was raised by Les Jackson of the United Kingdom in 1998. It is an extremely attractive maroon-red collerette dahlia with a white-tipped collar. Very good as a garden flower, as well as for cut flower use, this dahlia may yet prove its worth as exhibition material. Grows to a height of 1.1m (3½ft).

■ RIGHT

'JOMANDA'

As yet unclassified in the United Kingdom, this orange-blended, small-flowered ball dahlia was raised in the Netherlands by Cor Geerling and introduced in 1996. The blooms are fully petalled, reflexing well back to the long stems. Although back petals fade on maturity, this dahlia is excellent for show and cut flower purposes. Grows to a height of 1.2m (4ft).

■ LEFT

'KAREN GLEN'

Raised and introduced in 1990 in the United Kingdom by Gerry Woolcock, this extremely striking red miniature-flowered decorative is excellent for exhibition, garden and cut flower use, as it provides a wonderful profusion of blooms. For exhibition it requires special attention (double stopping) to maintain flower size. It has won many exhibitions throughout the world. Grows to a height of 1.2m (4ft).

■ ABOVE
'KENORA CHALLENGER'

One of a string of 'Kenora' varieties, this
pure white dahlia was raised by top breeder
Gordon Leroux in 1991 in the United
States. A contender for best-ever large-
flowered, semi-cactus, it is slim plant with
elegant blooms of massive depth –
definitely an exhibition flower. Grows to a
height of 1.2m (4ft).

■ RIGHT
'KENORA SUNSET'

This stunning bi-coloured, medium-
flowered, semi-cactus dahlia was raised
and introduced by Gordon Leroux in the
United States in 1996. Tall with brilliant
red-and-yellow blooms, this free-flowering
beauty is a must for gardens large enough
to accommodate it, and it is also good
for exhibiting. Grows to a height of
1.2m (4ft).

■ RIGHT

'KENORA VALENTINE'

Excellent for exhibition and garden use, this bright red large-flowered decorative was introduced by Gordon Leroux in the United States in 1990. Without attention, blooms tend to be oversize for exhibition use. Grows to a height of 1.2m (4ft).

■ LEFT

'KIDD'S CLIMAX'

Originally named 'Sir Edward', this pink-and-yellow blended decorative dahlia was raised by Ted Kidd in Dargaville, New Zealand, in 1940. A true giant-flowered dahlia in the United Kingdom when grown well and large-flowered in the United States, it is an exhibition legend, having won awards worldwide. Grows to a height of 1.1m (3½ft).

The Sheffield
College
Hillsborough LRC

■ ABOVE
'LEMON ELEGANS'

Cor Geerlings of the Netherlands raised this elegant pure
yellow, small-flowered semi-cactus dahlia in 1988. It possesses
deep, fully curving blooms on long stems, making it a good
grower for exhibition and garden use. Grows to a height of
1.1m (3½ft).

■ ABOVE
'KIWI GLORIA'

Eddie Durrant raised this small-flowered cactus dahlia in the
United Kingdom in 1988. A delicious lilac-and-white, late-
flowering variety, it is the top exhibition dahlia in the United
Kingdom. It must be stopped (centre removed) early to bloom for
shows. It makes a tall bush, but its thick stems and the fact that its
blooms grow low among the foliage render it unsuitable for garden
or cut flower use. Durrant has produced other small-flowered
cactus and semi-cactus varieties with the 'Kiwi' prefix; sports
include 'Deborah's Kiwi' (1996) and 'Trelyn Kiwi' (1997). Grows
to a height of 1.2m (4ft).

■ RIGHT
'LISMORE WILLIE'

Very tall growing, this orange-blended, small-flowered waterlily
dahlia, raised by Bill Franklin in the United Kingdom in 1992,
requires support. It is a prolific provider of exhibition, garden and
cut flowers on strong stems. Grows to a height of 1.5m (5ft).

■ LEFT
'MATCH'

This purple-and-white, small-flowered semi-cactus dahlia was raised in South Africa by A. Hindry in 1965. It was the forerunner of many other similar varieties. Outstanding as a garden variety due to its attractive and prolific blooms, this dahlia is also used in many a floral art exhibit. Grows to a height of 1.2m (4ft).

■ RIGHT
'MINLEY CAROL'

No list of dahlias would be complete without a 'Minley' pompon dahlia, 'Minley' being the prefix of Bill Wilkins who introduced the yellow-and-red blended 'Carol' in 1983. It is an excellent all rounder, good for exhibition, cut flower and garden use. The sport 'Red Carol' was introduced in 1994. Grows to a height of 1.1m (3½ft).

■ LEFT
'MOONFIRE'

Walter Jack of Invercargill, New Zealand, raised and introduced this single dwarf bedding dahlia in 1997. With orange-and-bronze blended blooms and bronze foliage, it is an excellent garden flower that is sure to be used in many parks and garden schemes together with 'David Howard'. Grows to a height of 75cm (2½ft).

'NARGOLD'

This medium-flowered semi-cactus, raised by
Cyril Higgo in South Africa in 1994, can be really
spectacular. The orange-and-gold petals are fimbriated
(laciniated), so the blooms are sometimes likened
to oversized carnations. With strong stems and
outstanding blooms, 'Nargold' is excellent for garden
or exhibition use. Grows to a height of 1.2m (4ft).

'PASO DOBLE'

Derek Hewlett discovered this
anemone dahlia in 1996, growing
in a municipal park in Germany. Its
profuse flowers, borne on long stems,
have white outer petals with a raised
yellow centre cushion. It produces
excellent tubers. Grows to a height
of 1.1m (3½ft).

■ RIGHT

'PHILL'S PINK'

This pink-and-yellow blended, small-flowered decorative of waterlily form was raised and introduced by Jack Kinns in the United Kingdom in 1970. Being long-stemmed, it is excellent as a cut flower as well as good for garden use. Grows to a height of 1.2m (4ft).

■ LEFT

'PINK PASTELLE'

In 1991 Tom Pashley in the United Kingdom raised this pink sport of 'Grenidor Pastelle', a pink-and-yellow blended medium-flowered semi-cactus (raised by John Carrington, United Kingdom, in 1988). Other 'Grenidor Pastelle' sports include: J. Newman's 'Gill's Pastelle' (1996), pink and white; and 'Pim's Pastelle' (1998), almost white-pink. The 'Grenidor' and 'Pink' varieties have proved to be regular show winners as well as garden and cut flowers, whilst 'Gill's Pastelle' and 'Pim's Pastelle' are beginning to prove useful. In a really sunny growing season the petals tend to split unevenly. Grows to a height of 1.2m (4ft).

■ BELOW

'PIPER'S PINK'

Raised in the United Kingdom in 1964 by Pipers, which is a nursery of long standing, this small-flowered, semi-cactus dahlia has long been grown successfully as dwarf bedding in parks and gardens everywhere. Its vibrant pink blooms have made it popular for garden and cut flower use. Grows to a height of 45cm (18in).

■ ABOVE

'PORCELAIN'

John Crutchfield raised and introduced this small-flowered waterlily dahlia in the United Kingdom in 1969, since which time it has proved a continuing success for cut flower use. The white-and-lilac blended blooms are borne on long, strong stems. Although very tall, it can also be used in the garden. Grows to a height of 1.5m (5ft).

■ RIGHT

'REMBRANDT'

Raised by Adrian and Cees Verwer in the Netherlands in 1997, this is an extremely eye-catching Gallery dwarf bedding dahlia with cream-tipped pink petals. It has proved to be excellent for border or patio use. Grows to a height of 25–30cm (10–12in).

■ RIGHT

'RENOIR'

Another Gallery dwarf bedding dahlia raised by Adrian and Cees Verwer in the Netherlands in 1997, this is deep pink but with more open petals than 'Rembrandt'. Excellent for border or patio use. Grows to a height of 25–30cm (10–12in).

■ BELOW

'SKIPLEY SPOT'

Introduced by R. Williams in the United States in 1989, this small-flowered decorative variety is red with uniformly white-tipped petals. A striking dahlia for garden use. Grows to a height of 1.2m (4ft).

■ ABOVE

'SMALL WORLD' (SYN. 'BOWEN')

Introduced in 1967 by Norman Williams of Australia, this white pompon has an occasional purple fleck, which may one day lead to a sport. It is excellent for exhibition and also good for garden and cut flower use. Grows to a height of 90cm (3ft).

■ RIGHT
'SO DAINTY'

A miniature-flowered semi-cactus dahlia introduced in 1971 in the United Kingdom by E. Richards, this exhibition variety with blooms of bronze blends is excellent for garden and cut flower use. It makes a compact bush. Grows to a height of 90cm (3ft).

■ LEFT
'TAHITI SUNRISE'

G. Cox raised this medium-flowered semi-cactus in the United Kingdom in 1975. A striking bi-colour yellow with red tipping, it is very useful for garden or cut flower use. A tall grower, it is better used at the back of a border. Grows to a height of 1.2m (4ft).

■ ABOVE

'TALLY HO'

A newer American lookalike for 'Bishop of Llandaff' that
is yet to be classified in the United Kingdom, this is red
with dark coppery, almost black, foliage. It is tall for a
peony type dahlia. Grows to height of 90cm (3ft).

■ RIGHT

'TARATAHI LILAC'

As yet unclassified in the United Kingdom, this lilac,
small-flowered cactus dahlia from New Zealand was
raised by John Frater in 1996. In the United Kingdom
it is a classic for cut flower and garden use, while in the
United States and New Zealand it is a universal winner
on the show bench, particularly when used in baskets.
It is prolific and easy to grow. Grows to a height of
1.2m (4ft).

■ RIGHT

'WESTON PIRATE'

This striking, dark-red, miniature-flowered, semi-cactus dahlia was raised by Tom McLelland in the United Kingdom in 1998. It is an excellent garden variety that is starting to succeed on the show bench. It is tall for a miniature. Grows to a height of 1.2m (4ft).

■ LEFT

'WHITE MOONLIGHT'

This is a white sport of the yellow parent 'Eastwood Moonlight' that was produced in 1984, with slightly smaller blooms. It can be susceptible to marking in seasons of mists and heavy dews. It forms a compact bush. Grows to a height of 1.1m (3½ft).

■ RIGHT

'WILLOW'S SURPRISE'

Introduced by Norman Williams in 1964, the longevity of this red-bloomed pompon dahlia as a show variety is matched only by its travels around the world. An exhibition variety that is also at home in the garden. Grows to a height of 90cm (3ft).

The Grower's Guide

Buying dahlias

Getting good results from dahlias starts with acquiring a good stock. Always buy the best and propagate only from the best of the best. First, ask yourself what you want from your dahlias. Do you want a garden display, cut flowers, or do you want to become an exhibitor? What you decide should influence what you buy. Second, consider the facilities you have access to. Whether you have a heated greenhouse, a coldhouse or a garden frame should govern your decisions.

Before you buy, look around. If you are not already a member of a horticultural society, join one; better still, try and find a specialist dahlia society to enrol with. Seek out a good grower, ask questions and read all you can – there are many books and some videos available. Be prepared to make mistakes, but learn from them.

Tubers

Most first-time dahlia buyers either visit a garden centre to buy dahlias, or see an offer for pre-packed tubers (the underground, fleshy roots of the plant) at a local supermarket. Pre-packed tubers are pot tubers, that is tubers that come from plants that have been grown in 13cm (5in) pots to restrict growth and produce good firm tubers.

This is not a bad way to start, and most of the tubers are very good, but the varieties widely marketed are often those that make good tubers, rather than the best flowers. Examine the contents carefully before parting with any money. If the tubers are soft, reject them. If there are buds developing, it is safe to buy. Read the description to make sure the contents are what you really want. Sadly, not all descriptions are correct and although the bloom on the label may show pink and white, yellow flowers may emerge.

■ ABOVE
A heated green-house plays an important part in successful propagation of dahlia plants.

■ LEFT
What you should look for when buying tubers: a healthy pot tuber (left) and a healthy tuber (right).

Tubers bought this way need a good start in life, preferably in a greenhouse or garden frame, and often do not respond to being planted directly in the ground – there is nothing a slug likes better than the first bite of the first shoot on a dahlia tuber. Buy tubers in early spring.

Plants

Dahlia plants can be bought from many good garden centres as well as specialist nurseries which provide a whole range to choose from, including collections. Also, many horticultural societies, especially dahlia societies, raise funds by selling members' surplus stock.

When buying a plant, choose a sturdy specimen with uniform distance between leaf joints; reject anything spindly. The plant should look vibrant and be bursting with vitality. Never

buy plants with mottled leaves, particularly one with minimal space between leaf joints which could indicate that the plant is harbouring a virus. Try to check the root ball. The roots should still have room to grow in the pot. Reject a root ball that is soggy or dried out; somewhere in between is what you want. If you are in doubt about any plant, do not buy it.

Depending on what care facilities you have, you can buy plants throughout spring. You can plant direct from purchase, but you must ensure that the plants are protected from frost. Where frosts occur late in the season, it may be safer to delay planting out until all danger of frost has past.

Visit nurseries as well as trial grounds in order to acquaint yourself with the plants and to appreciate the height, size of bush and growth habit of those varieties that appeal to you.

What varieties to buy and how best to use dahlias in your garden are also questions you need to satisfy yourself about. Dahlias are effective in beds where massed colours of red, pink or yellow are used in blocks, particularly if varieties with bronze or black foliage are used. Alternatively, if used in conjunction with salvias, petunias, non-stop begonias, *Verbena rigida* (syn. *V. venosa*) and *Senecio cineraria*

(syn. *Cineraria maritima*) with blooms of contrasting colours, the combination of the colour schemes will be superb. These arrangements have the advantage that planting schemes can be changed annually.

There was a time when no respectable municipal park or garden in the United Kingdom, particularly in seaside towns, would fail to have large bedding displays which inevitably included either a bed of dahlias or a combination of dahlias with other plants. This is in decline because of the pressure on local authorities to decrease costs. However, many British stately homes and gardens open to the public still feature dahlias in their bedding displays.

Readers with access to the world wide web can log on to 'Dahlia' on any search engine where some 900,000 dahlia references will be found. The lists of nurseries, seed sellers and gardens are endless, and cover most countries throughout the world.

Growing dahlias

■ BELOW LEFT
Straw is used to protect against frost.
■ BELOW
Tubers are dusted with fungicide.

There are three methods of propagating dahlias: sowing seed, dividing tubers (the fleshy, swollen roots of the plant) or taking cuttings. What you do will depend on the resources you have. Most established growers use all three methods at some time and sometimes all three in the same year.

Label plants that have produced the best blooms (stock selection) and save the tubers from those plants to propagate from them the following spring. 'Saving' means keeping them safe over winter. Tubers can be damaged by frost, but usually a 2.5cm (1in) layer of straw, peat or soil drawn over the dahlia bed will be sufficient protection in moderate climes. This layer can also incorporate slug pellets. Some growers lift tubers and store them over winter in greenhouses or sheds; if this is done, tubers should not be allowed to dry out.

After lifting tubers, stems should be cut to just above crown level (where main stem and fleshy tuber meet); this is where the next growing point or 'eye' should develop. Before final storage, place tubers upside down for a few days to allow any residual water in the stems or crown to drain away.

Protecting tubers

Prevention of mildew is essential. Use a proprietary fungicide, as directed by the manufacturers, dusting tubers and crown completely. Occasionally during winter inspect for mildew.

You can 'clamp' the tubers outside by protecting them with straw, and covering the whole heap with soil; however retrieval can prove difficult. In a greenhouse, make a clamp under the bench or in a box by covering a layer of polythene with wood shavings (more pest-free than straw), then tubers, more wood shavings and so on, remembering to add last any that need an earlier start than others. The clamp needs to breathe, so do not cover the shavings. The tubers should come out plump, and should be drenched in fungicide at once as any mildew spores will become active as soon as you retrieve them.

MAKING A CLAMP INSIDE YOUR GREENHOUSE

1 Lay a sheet of polythene in a box and cover with a layer of wood shavings 5cm (2in) deep.

2 Ensure that the tubers are labelled, then lay them on the top of the first layer of wood shavings.

3 Add more wood shavings on top of the layer of tubers. Continue layering tubers and shavings until all are covered.

Propagating from seed

Growing from your own seed can be fun because you never know what gift nature is going to bestow – it's down to the bees and other insects. Dahlias are virtually self-sterile, so they require other dahlias close by to ensure seed formation. Bees tend to go directly from one plant to the next, so similar varieties planted together tend to produce seeds for similar blooms, but this is not guaranteed. You should wait until the seed heads are entirely ripe before harvesting, and then allow them to dry prior to collecting the seed. Pull the seed head apart gently, ensuring that you catch everything in a container. Sort the seed from the rest of the dried seed head by winnowing (blowing or fanning the chaff from the seed). Be careful not to blow too hard or you could end up blowing everything away.

Dahlia seed is also available from some nurseries and garden suppliers. Usually this is a proprietary mix such as 'Coltness Gem' or 'Redskin' which will produce bedding scheme plants, but some specialist dahlia suppliers also market fully double seeds.

Sow the seed from mid-spring onwards in shallow trays containing a seed compost. Press the seed into the compost and sprinkle with a light covering of the compost. Make sure it is moist but not sodden, and place a piece of glass or polythene on top of the tray to prevent it from drying out. No further watering will then be needed before germination. Place a piece of newspaper over the glass on sunny days to protect the young seedlings. When the seedlings are about 7.5cm (3in) in height, pot them up and keep the young plants shaded for a few days if bright sun persists.

Harden them off by gradually reducing the glass covering, or moving them outside during the daytime, before finally planting out.

If you are trying to raise double dahlias, cactus, decorative, or whatever, remember the experts grow about 3,000 seedlings to get three acceptable varieties and then throw two away the following year or next. They are, of course, looking for perfection!

GROWING DAHLIAS FROM YOUR OWN SEED

1 Collect seed heads from late autumn onwards when they are fully ripe (left) and allow them to dry (right).

2 Pull the petals from the dried seed head. Blow away the unwanted parts and store the seed in labelled envelopes.

3 Sow the seed from mid-spring onwards in trays of moist seed compost, covering them thinly.

4 Pot seedlings into 7.5cm (3in) pots when they have grown to about 7.5cm (3in) in height.

Propagating from tubers

If you do not have a greenhouse, the tubers are best left in the ground until spring. Then, preferably in a dry spell, lift them from the ground, forking all round to free them so as to cause minimum damage. New fibrous roots will grow from the end of each tuber provided this is still attached to the crown. Semi-detached tubers or those with damaged ends will not provide the start in life required for new vigorous growth. Once a clump of tubers is above ground it can be divided with a sharp knife, hacksaw blade or spade ensuring that a new shoot, or eye, is attached to each tuber that is being removed. Without an eye, a tuber is 'blind' and no new growth will result. Given a generous clump, six or seven new plants can be achieved from digging up one parent plant. Parent tubers used this way are known as field tubers: they were grown in open ground the previous year. The new tubers produced from dividing the clump are known as 'fingers' in the United Kingdom or as 'chicken legs' in the United States.

'Setting up' tubers

Dahlias are tolerant propagators. Place or 'set up' the established tubers (tubers stored in the clamp over the winter or tubers that have been dug up in spring) in trays about 10cm (4in) deep, or directly onto a bench if you have a greenhouse, provided it is boxed along the sides to the same depth as the trays. Fill the trays with a peat or a soilless compost mixture. Before plunging the tubers into the compost, dip

HOW TO PROPAGATE FROM TUBERS

1 Lift tubers from the ground. When removing the clump of tubers, fork carefully all round to free them so as to cause minimum damage.

2 Once you have dug the tubers from the ground, gently clean the excess soil from them. Ensure that you label the tuber for later identification.

3 Divide up each tuber using either a sharp knife or a spade. It is vital that you make sure each tuber has an eye attached to it.

them in a bucket of hot disinfectant mixture. This will ensure that any residual bacteria or pests are destroyed before the tubers are 'plunged' into the compost. Ensure that the compost mixture is thoroughly moist before plunging the tubers into it. Do not plunge them too deeply into the mixture, however, because otherwise there is the danger that the crown may rot, which is something that should be avoided at all costs if you want to have healthy shoots. Make sure that the crown of each tuber is above the damp compost as this is where the new shoots will appear from. If at all possible, provide heat from below the trays of tubers, using an electric soil cable or paraffin or gas heater. You could also heat the compost for a few days beforehand.

Spray the compost with water for about a week, after which time new shoots should start to grow from the crown. At this point you should pot each tuber up separately, using general purpose compost, ensuring that each one has at least one shoot. The shoots that result from each of these tubers can be grown on as they are to produce new plants, or cuttings can be taken from them (see Propagating from cuttings section).

The method of propagating from pot tubers is slightly different to that of field tubers. They are too small to divide into 'fingers' as their growth has been restricted, unlike field tubers, but can be grown on in trays, and used for cuttings (see Propagating from cuttings section).

4 In this close-up view, the eye can be seen just to the left of the knife blade. New shoots will eventually be produced from the eyes.

5 Fill trays 10cm (4in) deep with moist, soilless compost and plunge the tubers shallowly into the surface, remembering to label the trays.

6 Spray the compost regularly for at least a week, by which time new shoots should have appeared. These can then be used for cuttings.

Propagating from cuttings

Instead of growing whole new plants from tubers, cuttings can be taken from tubers that have been grown for that purpose, or from leaves of established plants.

Moderation is the key when taking any sort of cuttings. Take only a few cuttings from each plant; taking too many will weaken the parent plant, and the resulting cuttings may be also be weak and less disease-resistant. If you are taking cuttings from tubers, keep tubers from each variety you wish to propagate, and take cuttings only from the first three shoots that each tuber produces. The resulting plants will then be strong and healthy.

Cuttings from shoots

Tubers that are to be used to produce new shoots should be placed in a box or tray of compost 10cm (4in) deep. Ensure that the compost is kept moist, and after about a week, shoots should start to appear from the eye of the tubers.

You can then begin to take cuttings. Use healthy shoots that have at least two pairs of leaves. Cut them off just below the second leaf joint, and remove the lower leaves. The end of each cutting should be dipped in a proprietary hormone rooting powder or liquid and be placed firmly, either individually or in batches, into pots or trays containing moist compost or a mixture of peat and sharp sand. Remember to label with the name of the variety; it is useful for record purposes to add the date when the

HOW TO PRODUCE NEW SHOOTS

1 Set up the tubers in a tray of compost filled about 10cm (4in) deep, remembering to label each one.

2 Cut shoots that have at least two pairs of leaves, cutting them off just below the second leaf joint.

3 Remove the lower leaves from each cutting. These will form the new dahlia plants.

4 Dip the end of each of the cuttings into proprietary hormone powder, following the manufacturer's instructions.

5 Plant cuttings in pots or trays that contain a moist mixture of peat and sharp sand. Label the pots.

6 Cuttings should root within ten days in a greenhouse environment. Ensure the compost is kept moist.

cutting was taken. Kept moist and with a greenhouse temperature maintained at 10°C (50°F), the cuttings should root after about ten days. Movement of air during this time will help to prevent 'damping off' (rotting) during rooting. If you do not have a greenhouse, cover the pots loosely with plastic bags and keep in a warm, light place. Remember that cleanliness is vital to avoid 'damping off', the spread of virus or infestation of aphids.

When rooted, each cutting requires a container about 7.5cm (3in) in diameter filled with a good compost. Once the cutting's roots fill the 7.5cm (3in) pot, they should be moved to a 13cm (5in) pot containing a multi-purpose compost.

Taking leaf cuttings

Pare a leaf with an axil bud (this is a bud that is produced in the joint between the leaf and stem node) from the parent plant, together with a tiny part of the stem; continue as with a cutting taken from a tuber, as described earlier.

Growing cuttings

Cuttings are best grown in a greenhouse environment, one that is moist and damp, but it is also possible to grow cuttings in a cellar without heat but under lights. Most cellars have a steady temperature that will suit dahlias, provided light and moisture are available.

SPORTS

Watch out for 'sports' in your garden. A sport occurs when, say, a red variety produces a pink bloom on one or more stem. Take leaf cuttings from these plants and grow as long as possible so as to obtain a tuber, however small. You can name this unique new variety after a friend or relation, or even a favourite football star.

■ ABOVE

The Magson family of sports have all originated from the same parent (left to right): Mary (yellow), Andrew (red) and Jackie (orange).

TAKING LEAF CUTTINGS FROM PLANTS

1 Cut off a leaf from the parent plant that has an axil bud together with a small amount of stem.

2 Dip each cutting into a proprietary hormone rooting powder and plant into pots, as described earlier.

Success with blooms

■ BELOW
Once the ground has been prepared, mark out the bed. Ensure there is adequate space for the plants to grow.

Success in growing dahlias depends on good ground husbandry. Dahlias grow best in water-retaining soil. Ideally, dahlias need a bed of their own to achieve their best, or at least a dedicated section within a herbaceous border. This is because the plant's rooting system can radiate up to 90cm (3ft) from the main tuber, and the fine, hair-like roots growing from the tubers cannot compete with more robust roots.

■ BELOW
Once the ground has been prepared, mark out the bed. Ensure there is adequate space for the plants to grow.

Preparation

Ground preparation should start in late autumn, after the previous season's plants have been cleared. The ground should be roughly dug. All types of soil will benefit from incorporating garden compost, or well-rotted manure if available, into the top spit (the depth of soil that can be dug up by pushing a spade into the ground and lifting and turning it over). This is done by throwing forward the rough lumps of soil to expose as much soil surface as possible to winter's elements. Double digging is not necessary.

In early spring, in dry conditions, fork over and rake the soil to complete the ground preparation. This is the time to add organic fertilizers, bonemeal or other proprietary products by lightly hoeing them in, or following the manufacturer's instructions. Frost is the enemy of dahlias, so weather conditions will dictate when to plant out. Dahlias can and do recover when cut down to ground level by frost, but not always. When they do recover, they bloom later. Before planting out the new plants, be sure to mark out the bed with stakes or

PREPARING THE GROUND

1 Roughly dig the ground over, throwing forward as much earth as possible to expose the soil surface to winter's elements.

2 In early spring, add organic fertilizers or other proprietary products to the soil, then hoe them in.

canes, leaving adequate space between plants so that they have room to grow – usually the space should be 60cm (2ft). However, the bigger the bloom required, the larger the distance needed between plants. Since dahlias vary considerably in height, check the expected growing heights of each variety, and make sure smaller ones will not be hidden.

Ideally, plant out during a dry period to prevent compression of the soil. Use a hand trowel to scoop out a hole, and plant the plants slightly lower than the surrounding soil, so a hollow is created which will retain water after watering during dry spells. They should be watered again a few days later if no rain occurs.

Dahlias require plenty of water, particularly during flowering, especially if they are being grown for exhibition. Remembering to attach a label on the cane or stake top, as well as in the ground at the bottom, when planting out will pay dividends in the autumn when you want to retrieve the best plant of the best variety.

Once the plants are well established, mulch around the plants when the bed is thoroughly moist, to retain the moisture and also to prevent the growth of weeds.

The mulch may be garden compost or well-rotted farmyard manure, although spent mushroom compost is an excellent alternative. Before acquiring a mulch, it is a good idea to find out if the supplier has used any undesirable chemicals that could have adverse effects on the plants.

As the plants grow, it is a good idea to add two additional support canes to each plant. Twine can be fixed to these to assist the stems and blooms against the ravages of wind and rain that can occur in most gardens, once summer has passed its high noon.

PLANTING OUT NEW DAHLIA PLANTS

1 Plant out the plants, so that they are slightly deeper than the level of the surrounding soil.

2 Add two extra canes to each plant to give more support as they begin to grow.

3 Twine can be fixed onto the canes to give more stability to each plant in case of wind and rain.

4 You can also attach mesh to the canes which will provide excellent support for the blooms.

Encouraging blooms

Once a plant is well established, the growing centre should be removed to encourage side breaks to occur. This practice is known as 'disbudding' or 'stopping'. When and how you do this depends on what you want from the dahlia. If you want early blooming for the garden or cut flowers, remove the centre when the plant has established itself, and is starting a period of rapid growth. This usually takes place about two to three weeks after the plant is planted in the ground. Removing the growing centre will encourage the plant's growth to be channelled into the resultant branches rather than into the central stem. If you are growing for shows, the best time to do it all will depend on many factors, including the weather, the location and the variety of the plant. With experience, you will be able to judge the best time in each

case. A sunny spring means a warmer bed, which together with good rainfall after planting will ensure sturdy, early growth, so this will tend to mean you can stop the plants earlier than you would in a cold season.

Each side break will normally produce a branch terminating in a main flower bud plus one or two ancillary, or side, buds, all of which will flower. If the side buds are removed, the main flower bud will produce a larger bloom. Similarly, each leaf axil on each stem will produce another shoot which, if left alone, will result in a further ancillary stem; this in turn will produce another flower stem with a main bloom plus ancillary blooms. Therefore, if you want many blooms, let them all mature. If you are seeking quality rather than quantity, remove all side buds and most leaf axial shoots, but not all.

USEFUL BLOOMS

Dwarf bedding types are useful for edging mixed flower beds, or varieties like 'Coltness Gem' for window boxes. Dwarf bedders apart, dahlias do not grow well in tubs or pots. They are best planted out in beds, where they are equally effective on their own or mixed with other plants. However, patio types bred mainly in the Netherlands and New Zealand are now becoming available; these compact plants grow very successfully in tubs.

■ ABOVE
Dwarf bedder 'Geerling's Indian Summer' adds a splash of colour.

'DISBUDDING' OR 'STOPPING' PLANTS

1 When the plant is well-established, remove the central shoot.

2 The side buds should be left intact and will produce blooms.

3 For just a few large blooms, remove most of the side shoots.

Cutting blooms

Dahlias can be cut with long stems, ideally just above one of the leaf axil buds, and this bud will become the next main bloom, probably in about 14 days. As dahlias provide blooms in abundance, you can repeat the process from, say, a late summer flowering until an early winter date. It is important that you always have a container of water ready when cutting dahlia blooms, so you can plunge them into the water the instant they are cut. Cut them early or late in the day, never in full sun.

Dahlias are enthusiastic drinkers, whether cut or on the plant, and the take-up of water affects the size of blooms. The size of a bloom will increase even after it has been cut and placed in water (a 15cm/6in bloom may increase in size by ½cm/¼in).

Cut stems with a diagonal slash to maximize stem contact with the water. Some dahlias have very hollow stems, especially giants and small decoratives. Pierce such stems below the water line to release trapped air and allow an increased take-up of water which will prevent back petal droop.

■ RIGHT
It is thought that ultra-violet rays are the cause of dahlia blooms' occasional strange colouration, although no laboratory trials have yet proven this.

CUTTING DAHLIA BLOOMS

1 Dahlias require plenty of water, so when you cut blooms, always ensure that you have a container of water ready.

2 Plunge the blooms into the water as soon as they have been cut; never leave them out of water once cut.

3 Using a sharp blade, make a diagonal slash on the stem to maximize the amount of water it is in contact with.

4 Pierce hollow stems below the water line to release trapped air, increasing the amount of water taken up.

UNUSUAL BLOOMS

Dahlia blooms sometimes do strange things, such as changing colour or producing a bloom with coloured halves or quarters. This colouration is believed to be the result of ultra-violet ray action during a previous growing season.

Exhibiting dahlias

Exhibiting dahlias can be an addiction and requires dedication, experience, experimentation and knowledge. To follow are a few tips for the exhibition beginner as well as those wanting to grow better blooms.

Plant pompons early. For some varieties, the second flush – the second flowering – produces better blooms. With all varieties of pompon, assist nature by removing the outer green calyx when the bud is showing colour; pinch the calyx leaves between your thumbnail and index fingernail to remove them. Long, sharp fingernails are very helpful for this. At first you may remove the whole bloom, but practice will help you perfect the technique. When growing pompons for exhibition, leave the centre bud to grow, unless the stem is not very long. In this case, remove the centre bud, allowing a side bud to flower, which should happen about ten days later. For most varieties of pompon, all the side buds should be removed.

With other types, disbudding of stems and debranching of plants is necessary to restrict the number of blooms on each plant – normally no more than three blooms on giants, four on large and six on mediums. With a larger size of bloom comes

HOW TO PRODUCE EXHIBITION-STANDARD POMPON BLOOMS

1 For a longer stem on pompons, remove the plant's centre bud, allowing a side bud to flower.

2 To ensure that the bloom reflexes fully back on to the stem, remove the calyx (the green casing of the bud).

diminished resistance to rain and sun, necessitating temporary covers, either large or individual. In the United Kingdom these are usually made of plastic to keep off rain. In the United States and New Zealand they are usually made of cheesecloth to keep off the sun.

Successful exhibiting is a result of good husbandry and cultivation, combined with ruthlessness in which there is no room for sentiment. If a variety is no longer seen as exhibition material, it should be discarded. Thorough preparation of soil and

plants is essential. Having completed a good regime, there are a few standard rules. Read the show schedule thoroughly, and make sure you know the current classification of your intended entry (all national societies issue classification regulations). Ensure that you are exhibiting your blooms in the right class. On the day, make sure the blooms are firmly secured to limit damage during transit – this is a frequent cause of disappointment. Ensure that you have all the equipment you need, including a

4 The best blooms often come from the second flowering, so plant early to ensure that you get a second 'flush'.

■ BELOW
A bunch of dahlias, of mixed or similar varieties, can make a wonderful splash of colour.

3 To remove the calyx, pinch the leaves firmly between the nails of your thumb and index finger.

sharp knife, tweezers, cotton buds and a small paint brush. When you arrive, take time to think what you are doing – don't get carried away by the heady show atmosphere. You can use the tweezers to remove any damaged petals, and replace adjacent petals with the brush or cotton buds. What the judge does not see, he or she cannot mark down. Finally, accept that there will be occasions when you will win when you shouldn't have done, and lose when you should easily have won: judges are only human.

■ BELOW LEFT
Crown gall on a tuber.
■ BELOW
Leaves infected with virus.

Diseases and pests

Dahlias are no different from other garden plants where diseases and pests are concerned. The old adage 'prevention is better than cure' is appropriate and should be observed all year round – during winter storage, during plant propagation and during the growing season. The following are some of the most common that you are most likely to encounter.

Diseases

Fungal infections

How to identify: In humid growing conditions, dahlias are susceptible to fungus infection. This shows itself as a leaf spot which starts as a small light green spot, increasing in size, turning yellow and eventually brown before dying off.
Cause: Infected spores are splashed up from the ground either by rain or by watering the plant's lower leaves.
Control and prevention: Burn any dead leaves, and then use a good proprietary fungicide on both the leaves of the infected plant and the surrounding soil to prevent further infection.

Galls

How to identify: Clumps of wartlike growths occasionally appear on leaves, or more particularly on the 'crown' of the tuber (where the tuber meets the stem).
Cause: Gall is caused by an infection from soil bacterium which enters the plant tissue where damage has occurred. The plant's cells are then stimulated to multiply rapidly. This usually occurs on the crown and eyes of the plant and results in the plant producing masses of cauliflower-like shoots instead of developing normally.
Control and prevention: If you absolutely have to grow this plant, remove the clump and grow on but do not propagate from the area of the gall. Infected tubers are really best destroyed.

Viruses

How to identify: 'Dahlia mosaic' is the commonest of all the viruses, and appears as mottled or distorted leaf patterns. Pale green-and-yellow markings produce a mosaic appearance. The virus dwarfs the infected plant, reducing its final height to 30cm (12in), often blistering the underside of the leaves. 'Cucumber mosaic' is another, not quite so virulent, virus imported from the cucumber. Again mottling of the leaves identifies the culprit. 'Spotted wilt virus', as its name implies, causes the plant to wilt, in addition to variegated leaf markings.
Cause: Viruses are spread by the sap of an infected plant entering the cells of a non-

infected plant. This occurs when a sucking insect (or aphid) feasts on an infected plant and moves on to a non-infected plant. They can also be spread via cutting blades if cuttings are being taken from more than one tuber.
Control and prevention: A plant with a virus is a menace not only to your other plants but also to your neighbour's plants due to the method by which viruses spread. Although there are no known cures for viruses at present, there is much you can do to prevent other plants succumbing. First of all, pull up and burn any plants you suspect are infected. Ensure all equipment is thoroughly cleaned, especially between taking cuttings from different plants: the phrase 'good husbandry' cannot be repeated too often. The prevalence of viruses in dahlias has been dramatically reduced over the years with good husbandry by both amateurs and professionals, and some varieties are now virus-resistant. However, be sure that your plant actually has a virus! Some viral symptoms can be similar to those of red spider mite infestation.

■ LEFT
A blackfly-infested stem.

■ RIGHT
A highly effective earwig trap.

Pests

Aphids

How to identify: Greenfly, blackfly and whitefly are clearly visible on plants, mainly on young growth and under leaves. They can spread viruses, distort bloom buds or the development of florets and generally debilitate plants.
Control and prevention: These are real enemies of the dahlia, and must be kept under control by spraying an appropriate proprietary contact or systemic insecticide at ten-day intervals, on the underside of leaves.

Caterpillars

How to identify: Caterpillars come in all colours and sizes.
Control and prevention: Spraying with a systemic insecticide will eliminate them, regrettably eliminating also the adult moth or butterfly that they might have one day become. There is no easy ecological solution.

Earwigs

How to identify: Earwigs are another danger to the dahlia. They eat leaf and bloom and always seem to have an eye for a prize bloom. Their trademark is a series of small holes on leaves before buds appear.
Control and prevention: Earwigs seem immune to versions currently marketed. Traps of small pots fixed upside-down on top of canes, filled with straw or paper, have been effective in trapping earwigs since Victorian times and are still used; dispose of the trapped earwigs by dropping them into a container of paraffin or boiling water. Some exhibitors grease the stems of their prize blooms, but earwigs manage to climb up adjacent plants and cross over leaves. If hollow canes are used to support plants, paraffin can be squeezed into them with devastating effect on earwigs.

Molluscs

How to identify: Slugs and snails will devour with relish young or old plants, the former preferably, at any time of the year, mostly at night and during or after rain.
Control and prevention: There are many proprietary pellets of metaldehyde or liquid forms available. Always use as instructed. If you prefer something more ecologically sound, then a saucer of beer as an overnight trap is highly effective. Old pots and trays left around, especially if in a damp spot, are good over-wintering homes. So you should remove them!

Red spider mite

How to identify: The red spider mite is microscopic in size and brown in colour; they look red en masse. Left alone, they spin a sort of web across blooms. The first symptoms are yellowing of the lower leaves, which will then turn brown and crisp.
Control and prevention: Remove and burn infected leaves. If you do not, the mites will move on to higher leaves. They thrive in hot, dry spells, so a good remedy is to spray leaves profusely with water on both sides. You can also spray at ten-day intervals with a proprietary chemical insecticide. The mites lay eggs which hatch out after ten days, so killing the adults with the first spray is not enough. Unfortunately, red spider mites over-winter on tubers and adjacent trees so vigilance is required at all times. A spray of proprietary insecticide on adjacent trees and in the greenhouse or coldframe will be effective. However, infected plants do provide decent, if not perfect, blooms, and with care an outbreak can be eliminated from the dahlia patch over time.

Wasps

How to identify: Wasps are borers and they like the fleshy stem tissue of the plant for lining their nests; they also extract sugar. Wasps have a habit of returning to the same place so can weaken a stem until it wilts.
Control and prevention: Traps made from jars of sugar water or beer with a small hole pierced through the lid are simple, but highly effective.

Calendar

Mid-winter

Check stored dahlia tubers for signs of fungus attack, which usually appears as grey mould on the stem or crown. Cut out affected parts and treat with fungicide. If it was not done in the autumn, now is the time to clean and disinfect thoroughly the greenhouse, benching, trays and pots that you intend to use for propagation. Check any electric installations and gas heaters in the greenhouse.

Ensure all equipment used during the year is thoroughly cleaned.

Late winter

If you have a propagating system, set up your tubers to take early cuttings to produce early plants and early blooms. Examine each clump of tubers and remove any damaged or dead pieces as this is where rot will set

in. Roots will grow from the ends of the tubers, so leave these intact. Ensure the crown of the tuber is set above compost level. Maintain a night temperature of 10°C (50°F) and beware of slugs and snails.

Early spring

Take cuttings below the first pair of leaves, ensuring you do not damage the crown. Do not take too many cuttings from one tuber and pot cuttings on as soon as possible. Spray them in the morning and evening and protect from direct sunlight. If you are not taking cuttings, start looking in the local garden centre for early delivery of tubers, or lift the previous year's tubers from the bed ready for division and store in a frost-free place. Split field tubers of late-flowering varieties and grow on in pots or trays.

Mid-spring

Divide the previous year's tubers and place tubers with an eye in a suitable container of fresh compost. Depending on the weather, place new plants in a frost-resistant cold frame to 'harden off'. Liven up the dahlia plot by raking, forking or rotovating the soil. Feed the soil by adding inorganic fertilizers to it.

Late spring

If you do not have a greenhouse, divide the previous year's field tubers and place split tubers in trays into a cold frame to increase stock. Set out canes or posts for planting positions, one cane per plant: make sure you allow plenty of space between canes. Plant out divided or purchased tubers. At the end of the season, plant out home-grown or purchased plants.

Early summer

Remove the growing centre of all plants. Hoe between plants to keep down emerging weeds, taking care not to damage any dahlia roots that are near to the surface. If this is a dry period, water regularly. Spray against insect pests and start to trap earwigs. The young appear now and every earwig killed now means less damage to your blooms. Start a watering regime: 95% of a dahlia is water, so if the weather is warm (around 20°C/70°F) each plant requires 9 litres (2 gallons) every other day.

Mid-summer

Mulch between plants with homemade or spent mushroom compost, farm manure, or straw, but only after

■ RIGHT
After the first frosts have occurred in late autumn, cut the plants down to just above ground level.

ensuring that the compost does not contain aphids or weedkiller residue, and that the plot is well watered. Mulching will retain moisture and prevent weed growth. After mulching, add additional support canes as necessary. Spray against insect pests on a weekly basis. Start to feed plants with a high-nitrogen liquid feed, following the manufacturer's instructions. Keep up the watering regime. Some early disbudding can be done to ensure longer stems for the blooms. Watch out for viruses and destroy affected plants.

Late summer

Dahlias require regular attention at this time. Growth can be spectacular and rapid at this time of year, and blooms can be lost through lack of attention. If you want to produce

■ ABOVE
Cutting plenty of blooms during the late summer encourages growth.

bigger blooms, disbud and debranch plants. Keep re-tying plants as branches are removed or blooms cut. If you are going to cover your blooms for exhibition purposes, check or erect the supports for the covering frames.

Early autumn

Identify and mark the plants producing the best blooms for propagation next year. Replace the liquid feed with a high-potash feed to improve tuber growth and retain strong stems. Continue protecting plants against pests. Cut blooms as required. Remove 'dead heads' unless you want to keep some for seeding. Maintain bloom quality by taking out thin side branches where main stems have been cut. Keep up the spraying and watering regime, although the latter can start to be tailed off.

Mid-autumn

Plants start to decline at this time of year. Continue spraying against pests as aphids are still around. Towards the end of this period, remove and clean canes before storing. Prepare to store tubers over winter: clean trays or boxes, peat or straw and other storage material should be ready. Have a supply of fungicide for dipping the tubers when lifting.

Late autumn

Cut down all plants to just above ground level, preferably soon after a frost. Remove debris for composting or burning. Burning disposes of any lingering pests and diseases. Lift tubers, ensuring in the process that labels stay attached to the correct tubers. Remove dead or damaged tubers. In a heated greenhouse or other frost-free store, store tubers in a peat or a similar protective medium. Otherwise, dig over a suitable plot and replant the tubers with at least 2.5cm (1in) of protection. Towards the end of the season, start the winter rough digging, adding well-rotted manure or compost. Be sure to expose as much soil surface as possible when rough digging.

Early winter

Complete the winter digging. If you are concerned about the soil's fertility, test the soil. Study the nursery catalogues you have collected and enjoy a well-earned rest, thinking of the all the blooms you will raise next season.

Other recommended dahlias

'Degas'

'Pink Giraffe'

'Kelsea Carla'

'Moorplace'

As well as those included in the Plant Catalogue, the following are also highly recommended. Everyone has a favourite dahlia, perhaps varieties that never made it in any category – garden, exhibition or cut flower – but mean something to those who originally grew them, or dahlias that did make it but have been overtaken by newer and better varieties. Each and every dahlia grower will have a list in mind.

'Bonny Blue'
Perhaps the oldest of garden dahlias still grown, it has also been known as 'Blue Danube'. It was raised in the United Kingdom in 1940 by Archer and is a lilac-blue, small ball dahlia whose blooms are prolific, but not the best of stem makers. It is a strong tuber producer. Grows to a height of about 75cm (2½ft).

'Degas'
Useful rich pink, Gallery,

dwarf bedding dahlia raised by Adrian and Cees Verwer in Holland in 1997. Excellent for border or patio use. Grows to a height of about 25–30cm (10–12in).

'Edinburgh'
Raised and introduced in Scotland in 1950 by Dobbies Ltd. Sometimes called 'Edina', this small, purple, white-tipped decorative is still a favourite in many gardens and is also used for floral art. Producing sturdy, reliable plants and blooms, it has now been overtaken by more modern varieties on the show bench. Grows to a height of about 90cm (3ft).

'Frontispiece'
A white, fimbriated (laciniated) giant semi-cactus that was raised and introduced by Bruidegom in Holland in 1962 (given away as a complimentary variety). In its day it was a spectacular exhibition variety. Grows to a

height of 90cm (3ft).

'Garden Party'
Raised by van Veelen in Holland in 1961, this small-flowered cactus dahlia has outlived many rivals. Free-flowering with orange-and-yellow blended blooms, it makes an excellent dwarf bedding plant. Grows to a height of 60cm (2ft).

'Giraffe'
Classified as miscellaneous, this double orchid dahlia was raised by Hoek in the Netherlands in 1948. Its bronze-and-yellow variegated blooms are extremely popular with floral artists. A pink sport was raised by Burrows in the United Kingdom in 1961. Both are excellent as cut flowers but stock is difficult to obtain because it is very vulnerable to viruses. Grows to a height of about 90cm (3ft).

'Hallmark'
A pink and light-pink blended pompon which is good for

garden, cut flower and exhibition use. Introduced in the United Kingdom in 1960. The centre petals of the bloom can be looser than other pompons and may need to have the side buds removed to achieve a 5cm (2in) diameter, but really superb when well grown. Grows to height of about 1.2m (4ft).

'Jennie'
This is a white-and-pink blended, medium semi-cactus from Phil Traf, a top United States raiser. Introduced in 1989, this is another fimbriated (laciniated) variety which is at home in the garden or on the show bench. 'Jennie' has excellent stems and produces prolific, good-quality blooms. Grows to a height of 1.1m (3½ft).

'Jescot Julie'
Raised in the United Kingdom in 1974 by veteran dahlia grower, E. Cooper, whose many 'Jescot' varieties were

'NZ Robert'

'Omo'

'Peachette'

'Pink Sensation'

regular small-flowered category successes in the 1960s and 1970s. 'Julie' is a double orchid type. An eye-catching burnt orange with a plum reverse, it is good for garden and cut flower use. Grows to a height of 90cm (3ft).

'Kelsea Carla'
As yet unclassified but raised and introduced in 1998 in the United Kingdom by Tony Hindle. This pink-and-yellow blended, small-flowered cactus dahlia should be excellent for exhibition, garden and cut flower purposes. Grows to a height of 1.2m (4ft).

'Klankstaad Kerkrade'
A sulphur-yellow small cactus raised in the Netherlands that was named after a local festival and introduced in 1954, this was the most popular dahlia for exhibitors during the 1960s. It is an excellent garden, cut flower and exhibition variety where size is not a factor. Sports include:

'White Klankstaad' (1967); 'Majestic Kerkrade' (1973), pink and yellow; 'Pink Kerkrade' (1987); and 'Lady Kerkrade' (1987), lavender and white. All exhibition winners, as well as good garden and cut flowers. Grow to a height of 90cm (3ft).

'Lavengro'
Lavender-and-bronze blended giant decorative introduced in 1953 by A.T. (Bertie) Barnes, the first of the modern great United Kingdom growers and raisers of giant dahlias. This variety blooms earlier than most giant decoratives and can be used for garden and exhibition but sadly has been surpassed by more modern varieties. The blooms go to sleep at night: the top half of the bloom folds over at dusk. Grows to a height of about 1.2m (4ft).

'Moorplace'
Named after a golf course in Surrey, United Kingdom, this

classic pompon dahlia was raised in 1957 by Alan Newnham. With rich royal purple, occasionally near black, blooms from mid-summer to late autumn, this is a winner for show, cut flower or floral art use. Treated well, it will hardly ever produce a bad bloom, but must be double-stopped from early produced plants to achieve best results. Grows to a height of 1.1m (3½ft).

'NZ Robert'
This red, lilliput-flowered dahlia was originally found in 1993 by Trevor Nixon of Timaru, New Zealand, in the garden of a recently deceased music teacher and dahlia grower, after whom it was named. It was found growing as a seedling, adjacent to a bed of lilliput dahlias. Sent to the 'Southdown' trials, it won the 1993 Takitimu award for garden excellence and was released by Walter Jack, Belle

Fleur Gardens, New Zealand. Producing a profusion of bright red flowers on a low plant, it is useful for bedding or patio tubs. Grows to a height of 45cm (18in).

'Omo'
Of uncertain age and origin, this single lilliput-flowered dahlia is white with a yellow disc. It is excellent for patio and pot use. Grows to a height of 45cm (18in).

'Peach Cupid'
This perfect pink-blended, miniature-flowered, ball dahlia is a 1993 sport of the pink 'Wootton Cupid' which was raised by Les Jones in Leek Wootton, United Kingdom in 1980. The prolific blooms on strong straight stems are excellent for exhibition, garden and cut flower purposes, and can be cut week after week throughout the flowering season. Needs time to mature and plenty of water if a green centre is to be avoided. Other

'Red Dwarf'

'Sir Alf Ramsey'

'Weston Pinkie'

'Wootton Cupid'

As well as those included in the Plant Catalogue, the following are also highly recommended. Everyone has a favourite dahlia, perhaps varieties that never made it in any category – garden, exhibition or cut flower – but mean something to those who originally grew them, or dahlias that did make it but have been overtaken by newer and better varieties. Each and every dahlia grower will have a list in mind.

'Bonny Blue'
Perhaps the oldest of garden dahlias still grown, it has also been known as 'Blue Danube'. It was raised in the United Kingdom in 1940 by Archer and is a lilac-blue, small ball dahlia whose blooms are prolific, but not the best of stem makers. It is a strong tuber producer. Grows to a height of about 75cm (2½ft).
'Degas'
Useful rich pink, Gallery,

dwarf bedding dahlia raised by Adrian and Cees Verwer in Holland in 1997. Excellent for border or patio use. Grows to a height of about 25–30cm (10–12in).
'Edinburgh'
Raised and introduced in Scotland in 1950 by Dobbies Ltd. Sometimes called 'Edina', this small, purple, white-tipped decorative is still a favourite in many gardens and is also used for floral art. Producing sturdy, reliable plants and blooms, it has now been overtaken by more modern varieties on the show bench. Grows to a height of about 90cm (3ft).
'Frontispiece'
A white, fimbriated (laciniated) giant semi-cactus that was raised and introduced by Bruidegom in Holland in 1962 (given away as a complimentary variety). In its day it was a spectacular exhibition variety. Grows to a

height of 90cm (3ft).
'Garden Party'
Raised by van Veelen in Holland in 1961, this small-flowered cactus dahlia has outlived many rivals. Free-flowering with orange-and-yellow blended blooms, it makes an excellent dwarf bedding plant. Grows to a height of 60cm (2ft).
'Giraffe'
Classified as miscellaneous, this double orchid dahlia was raised by Hoek in the Netherlands in 1948. Its bronze-and-yellow variegated blooms are extremely popular with floral artists. A pink sport was raised by Burrows in the United Kingdom in 1961. Both are excellent as cut flowers but stock is difficult to obtain because it is very vulnerable to viruses. Grows to a height of about 90cm (3ft).
'Hallmark'
A pink and light-pink blended pompon which is good for

garden, cut flower and exhibition use. Introduced in the United Kingdom in 1960. The centre petals of the bloom can be looser than other pompons and may need to have the side buds removed to achieve a 5cm (2in) diameter, but really superb when well grown. Grows to height of about 1.2m (4ft).
'Jennie'
This is a white-and-pink blended, medium semi-cactus from Phil Traf, a top United States raiser. Introduced in 1989, this is another fimbriated (laciniated) variety which is at home in the garden or on the show bench. 'Jennie' has excellent stems and produces prolific, good-quality blooms. Grows to a height of 1.1m (3½ft).
'Jescot Julie'
Raised in the United Kingdom in 1974 by veteran dahlia grower, E. Cooper, whose many 'Jescot' varieties were

The Sheffield College
Hillsborough LRC

Useful addresses

Dahlia societies

The National Dahlia Society (UK)
30 Glasbrook Drive,
Twickenham, Surrey, TW2 6AH
Tel. 0208 287 0031
www.dahlia.org.uk
The National Dahlia Society produces
*National Dahlia Societies Classified
Directory* which is updated and published
every two years.

American Dahlia Society
For membership information:
ADS Membership,
1 Rock Falls Court,
Rockville, MD 20854
Tel. 202 326-3516
www.dahlia.org
The American Dahlia Society publishes
an annual *Classification and Handbook
of Dahlias.*

Australian Dahlia Society
Although there is no overall classification
list produced due to distances and
climatic differences between states,
Growing Dahlias by Gaynor Parker is a
useful publication.

New Zealand Dahlia Society
General Secretary,
78 Cameron Road,
Te Puke
The classification of dahlias in New
Zealand is issued in *Dahlias in New
Zealand* which was started in 1990 by
Dr Keith Hammett.

Dahlia nurseries

United Kingdom
Aylett Nurseries
North Orbital Road,
St. Albans AL2 1DH
Tel. 01727 822255

Halls of Heddon,
West Heddon Nurseries
Heddon-on-the-Wall NE15 0JS
Tel. 01661 852445

Oscrofts
Spotborough Road,
Doncaster B93 0BP
Tel. 01302 785026

Taylors
12 Shawbury Grove, Sale,
Cheshire M33 4DF
Tel. 0161 973 7178

Winchester Growers
Winnall Down Farm,
Fair Lane, Winchester,
Hampshire SO21 1HF
Tel. 01962 853541

New Zealand
Belle Fleur Gardens
Northope, Invercargill
Tel. 03 2368523

United States
Connells Dahlias
10616 Waller Road East,
Tacoma, WA 98446
Tel: 253 531 0292

Pleasant Valley Glads & Dahlias
87 Edward Street, PO Box 494,
Aqawam, MA 01001

Creekside Dahlias
Route 4 Box 273, Ellijay, GA 60540

Bridgeview Dahlia Gardens
1876 Maple Street,
North Bend, OR 97459

The rich, vivid colours of dahlias make
a wonderful contribution to an informal
mixed border.

Index

ACKNOWLEDGEMENTS
All photographs by Jonathan Buckley, except: Ian Butterfield: 25br, 57tl, 60tml; Peter Cleaver: 62tml; Ted Collins: 56b; Garden Picture Library: 6–7, 8, 9b, 11bl, 12b, 13tr, 13bl, 14b, 33tl, 55b; Terry Gillam: 49br, 53b; Frank Newbery: 60tr.

■ 'Hamari Accord'

The Sheffield College